SHARED **READING** *SHARED* **WRITING**

CLPE

(London Borough of Southwark)
Centre for Language in Primary Education
Webber Row
London SE1 8QW

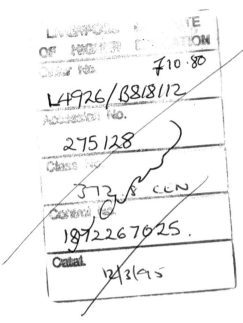

Contents

One, two, three four, five.
by I.T.

Ball wool
by I.T.

The Cold Winter Book
by I.T.

We found all these books about babies

THE WILD BABY

I Want My Potty

Introduction

Shared reading and shared writing are activities that have assumed considerable importance in primary classrooms over the last few years. By "shared reading" we tend to mean a group of children reading a "big book" – either commercial, or home-made – with the teacher; while "shared writing" is generally used to mean those occasions when a group composes a text together with the teacher acting as scribe, using a flip chart so that everyone can see the developing text. But of course, these meanings are not exclusive, and many of the pictures in this book show other kinds of situations where reading and writing are shared, or collaborative, activities, and where children are learning the social nature of reading and writing.

All reading and writing can be seen as essentially social even though they may appear to be solitary processes. Whenever we read a text we are, after all, sharing it with all its other readers, and when we write, we are writing for others to read. Children's early experiences can help them to realise that in becoming readers and writers they are joining a community of others who share their enjoyment – what Frank Smith calls the "literary club". This realisation can be of fundamental importance, and the activities which develop it, the creation of a range of opportunities for sharing reading and writing in the classroom in groups of all sizes, story time, collaborative writing, the publication and display of children's writing and the creation of audiences, the discussion of books and the sharing of reading choices, listening corners, the dramatisation of stories, all of these are ways in which the social nature of literacy is demonstrated daily. For young bilingual children, whose early literacy experiences are part of their learning of English, such demonstrations are particularly crucial.

In this book, contributors describe how they have used shared reading and writing in the classroom, and why they value it. Several of them refer to Don Holdaway's book *The Foundations of Literacy*, and this was certainly a key text in the movement that is now well established in many schools. Holdaway's work with enlarged texts offered a way of supporting inexperienced readers and allowing them to join in as much of the reading as they could manage, much as Liz Waterland's "apprenticeship approach" does. Holdaway also emphasised the value of sharing favourite books over and over again, with children taking on more and more of the reading for themselves. Teachers who have become dissatisfied with the linguistic and narrative experience provided in many reading schemes, have found in Holdaway's approach an alternative framework for the reading in their classrooms.

Undoubtedly the move to "real books", and the encouragement of children's early independent writing, have made shared reading and writing key features of modern classrooms. The information that children derive from these kinds of "demonstrations" can be basic to their developing understandings, while the communal nature of the experiences means that children can share their knowledge and achieve more than they could individually, or supported by the teacher in one-to-one situations. The articles in this book show something of the range of practice that can be included under this title, and why it is an important educational development.

Myra Barrs *CLPE*

Shared Reading and Shared Writing

Sue Pidgeon

Much 'shared reading' and 'shared writing' goes on in Primary classrooms today, but what does this actually mean? The term seems to have slipped into primary school terminology, alongside 'Baker Days' and 'Minibeasts', but the words themselves can describe a range of different activities, and are, in fact, far from self explanatory. Mention Shared Reading and Writing to anyone outside teaching, and they will give you a funny look! So now perhaps it is time to look again at Shared Reading and Shared Writing, to look at the origins of the ideas, and to see how teachers are using them in classrooms in many different ways, in order to help children learning to be literate.

The strength of Shared Reading and Writing for me is that through using real reading and writing opportunities and a collaborative approach the children are able to experience reading and writing 'for meaning' and to see how the reading and writing process works – that is, what readers and writers DO when they read and write. I suppose, in essence, Shared Reading or Shared Writing could be defined as 'a text that is shared among the participants for their mutual pleasure and understanding'. The text can be shared between the children themselves, or between a teacher and the children; the size of the group involved can range from two to the whole class. In fact one of its strengths is that there is no 'one' way of doing it!

So, WHY IS IT USEFUL AND WHERE DOES IT COME FROM?

It was Don Holdaway, working in New Zealand in the 1970's who first emphasised the role of Shared Reading for children learning to read. He was working with children already reading when they came into school in order to find out something about HOW children learn to read, and discovered that many of the children seemed to have used 'favourite stories' as their way into reading. These were stories that were read to them often and that the child enjoyed and understood.

Gradually the child was able to move away from being dependent on the adult and start to take on some of the reading themselves, firstly through remembering the text, and later through being able to match words and phrases to the text they knew.

He noted two important points from this. First that the child was helped by the adults, that they provided the 'scaffolding' that allowed the child to move gradually into taking reading on for themselves. Secondly, that because the children could SEE the book that was being read to them, they were able to learn about the story, about books and about print, and that this knowledge was crucial for enabling them to move into reading for themselves. If this approach was successful at home, he thought that it should be successful in school, but realised that it would not be feasible for each child to have the amount of one-to-one attention needed.

So he devised a way of making the books accessible to a wider audience. He took the books that were already the class favourites, and made enlarged versions so that a group of children could see them when they were being read aloud. Either the teachers wrote out the stories in the same page arrangement as the book and illustrated them, or they enlarged them on the photocopier. Then they read the enlarged books as they normally would to the children, but the children could now also focus on the book, the pictures, and the text, and could join in with the reading if they wanted to. He found it particularly successful in the classroom, and noted that it was possible, through the shared nature of the approach, for all the children to be successful. It did not matter whether a child was at the earliest stages of reading, and just becoming familiar with the sound of the story and the way the book worked, or if they were able to read the text themselves, they were all able to be involved in the 'shared reading' of an enjoyable text. (There is a very interesting account of this work in his book 'The Foundations of Literacy'.)

This provided the impetus for Shared Reading to become part of classroom practice; it seemed to introduce reading the 'right way round' by starting with the meaning rather than the words. It also introduced children learning to read to both sides of the process, firstly, to the content of a book or story, and then to features of the text (the words, letters, etc.), both of which are important to know in order to be a successful reader. The success in New Zealand was taken up in Britain.

It was while teachers on courses at CLPE were making enlarged versions of their classes' favourite books that a teacher noted that by involving the children in the 'shared writing' of a book, the children both enjoyed the collaborative task, and seemed to learn something about the writing process from it. Suddenly it seemed quite obvious that if shared reading helped reading development, so a similar approach to writing could help writing development.

Also by involving children in the writing of books that they can then read, it was possible to see the full circle of the literacy process, that writers produce texts for readers to read.

There is a further aspect to literacy development where shared reading and writing have a part to play and that is in helping to make the literacy process explicit to children. This also differentiates the present approach from any of its predecessors. Although in one sense there is nothing new about it – for example, it is similiar to the old 'class news' – the theoretical premises behind it are very different. It is now sometimes suggested that as a part of successful literacy development children may need to have a more 'explicit' knowledge of language.

This knowledge about language is known as 'metalinguistic awareness' and would seem to be an alternative to what Kenneth Baker calls 'grammar'. This is knowledge that children already have implicitly through their use of language (for example, although young children cannot tell you

writing process and what 'information' counts. Children who are not successful are not always sure about what they should be paying attention to in the text. In Shared Reading and Writing the teacher can point out the important features and children can learn from each other's observations.

But as well as looking at the role of Shared Reading and Writing in children's literacy development, I think it is also important to see it as part of a wider theory of learnng. We know that learning is most effective when it is collaborative, when learners work together and share their knowledge and resources. Research into learning has shown this for some time. For example, Piaget noted how much children learnt from one another, and the developmental psychologist Vygotsky considered that an essential part of learning is the co-operative and social nature of it. Through collaborative learning children can tackle things that are slightly beyond their present developmental stage.

Vygotsky calls this the 'zone of proximal development', and says "What the child can do in co-operation today, he can do alone tomorrow" So Shared Reading and Writing allows children to work on something together that they could not do individually. Because of the collaborative nature of learning, this means that Shared Reading and Writing are not only relevant to children who are at an early stage of learning to read and write but are in fact appropriate learning at all stages. This approach can be a particularly useful way of showing how language and literacy work, which means that it is particularly relevant for bilingual, learners as well as for monolingual learners.

Both 'learning' and literacy are social by nature. Although for many adults, reading and writing may be solitary activities, literacy is about communicating and generates a tremendous amount of discussion and talk, whether it be recommending a novel to a friend, a review of a new novel in the Sunday paper or arguing over the

phrasing of a document on 'School Policy'. The making of any text is a collaborative venture inasmuch as it involves editors, printers, publishers, etc. So again Shared Reading and Writing fit into this collaborative tradition.

So, how can it be organised in the classroom? I think the only essential point to make is that since it is about learning to be literate, it must be linked with real reasons for reading and writing. And so children need enjoyable books for shared reading and need to be 'shared writing' for real reasons and purposes. It is important that it keeps sight of what is involved in reading and writing and does not become an activity that is only relevant to school – like lining up, and 'Music and Movement'. But within it there are tremendous opportunities for a variety of uses in the classrooms, either with the children and the teacher working together, or with the children collaborating.

When the teacher and the children are working together, the teacher's role is that of 'demonstrating' what a reader or writer does, thus leaving the children to incorporate this knowledge into their knowledge about reading and writing and to act upon it in their own time. There are many different aspects of the reading and writing process; the teacher has scope to involve the children in the meaning of the 'whole', but also to focus on any 'parts' that may be relevant. This could be as simple as the way we read print from left to right, or as sophisticated as the spelling of 'photograph'.

Shared Reading has been used very successfully in Infant classrooms in the way Holdaway suggested; to introduce children to books and stories on a regular and consistant basis, so that the children build up a knowledge about books and stories, and a repertoire of favourite books that they know so well they can begin to 'read' themselves.

But Shared Reading is not limited to stories, it can be used with any texts: notices, information,

what a verb is, they know where to put one when they are talking and say "give me that book".)

Individual reading and writing experiences do not always lead to this knowledge, but shared reading and writing are useful because they seem to demonstrate the different elements of the reading and writing process. It is easy, for example, to point out question marks, or to talk about another way of saying 'he went', i.e. to talk about linguistic features. There is some evidence to suggest that part of successfully learning to read and write is making the right connections, realising what is important in the reading and poetry, letters, jokes, etc. It is often a good way to introduce a new kind of writing to children, and especially something like poetry which looks and sounds different from story writing. The best way to do any Shared Reading is always to read the text first, for the meaning, to or with the group, and then to discuss any particular aspect of it. It is important that the children can see the text they are reading, so for any group larger than two or three, you need to use an enlarged text.

Shared Writing works in the same way as Shared Reading, except that 'creating' a text involves more discussion and more argument! The teacher is taking on the chore of the writing, leaving the children free to contribute to the composition, and later to the transcription. Shared Writing needs to be approached like any writing task, allowing time to discuss the content, time to get the ideas down on paper and then time to re-read what has been written and revise if necessary. It is in the stage when the content of the completed text is re-read that the teacher can focus on a particular aspect of writing (for example, a full stop). Again there is scope for doing shared writing with small and large groups, with the only proviso being that the writing must be large enough for the children involved to read it easily.

Shared Reading and Writing with an adult are not confined to working with the teacher: parents, helpers and older children can act as 'the reader' for Shared Reading or the 'writer' for Shared Writing.

The other main way Shared Reading and Writing are used in the classroom is for children to work together on some reading and writing. This is a well established part of many classroom literacy programmes. Children read to or with one another, both informally, and also working on specific reading tasks like reading a play in a group, or reading and illustrating a story together. When children are writing together, they may collaborate on any kind of writing, and can take turns at being 'the scribe'. or remove this pressure completely by using the word processor or the computer. Children working together on literacy tasks in the classroom combine the good learning opportunities of collaborative learning with all aspects of literacy, talking and listening, reading and writing.

This seems to me to be the strength of shared reading and writing. They combine theory and practice in a manageable way. Children are using real literacy events for learning, and they are working together on a text. This is not a kit out of a box, or a rigid programme. It is a part of good primary practice with its roots in theory, but which allows teachers to use it in the way that is appropriate for them. I saw a nice example of this the other day: the teacher, as part of some class work on 'Wheels' had brought in a car tyre to an infant class. The children had done a lot of work with it, looked at the tread patterns, drawn it, washed it etc. and the teacher suggested that they should write to Kwik-fit to thank them. The task was a real one, a thank you letter for something they had enjoyed. The children made suggestions, the teacher wrote them down and at the end had a collaborative letter that said what they wanted to say, but that had also introduced them to a new kind of writing, a letter, with its distinctive layout. The letter was duly sent off. Together they had written a successful letter, and with more 'shared' letter writing, in time, they will be able to take this for of writing on themselves. This is surely what learning is all about.

Sue Pidgeon

References
Don Holdaway *The Foundations of Literacy* Ashton Scholastic 1979

Goodbye Peter, Goodbye Jane
Gillian Lathey

It took me ten years to wean myself from reading schemes. From the first realisation that abandoning Peter and Jane, Karen and Tommy, and even Johnny and Jennifer was a possibility, I wanted to do just that – but felt in desperate need of props. Liz Waterland in Read with Me (1987) describes how she temporarily lost her nerve when using 'real' books and reverted to 'Link-Up'. I felt that panic even before making the attempt! With hindsight I could now suggest several means of supporting a move away from schemes:– involving parents, getting to know books well in order to match them to children's needs, considering the child as an 'apprentice' reader (Liz Waterland, 1987) – and using 'big books'. These can both increase children's repertoire of stories and rhymes, and help to focus their attention on print.

'Big Books', both home-made versions of favourite stories and those comercially published, can provide an enjoyable group experience of story and rhyme. Children quite naturally 'chime in' and with time and much repetition the stories and rhymes then become part of the class 'folk memory'. Don Holdaway stresses this point in his consideration of the use of enlarged texts (Holdaway, 1979):

> 'We find that corporate experiences of culturally significant language have always been powerful modes of learning'.

Such learning is supported when children have access to the big books themselves and small versions of the texts, so that they can browse alone and indulge in the speculation and reflection which a group experience allows little time for.

Big books can play an important part in helping children to take on book language and to develop an awareness of language patterns, with the visual association of the text in front of them. It is often best to start with an enlarged version of one of the children's favourite stories or rhymes, thus ensuring their commitment. Brenda Tormey,

deputy head at Hugh Myddelton Infants School, has worked successfully with big books for some time, both large versions of class favourites and books composed by the children in shared writing sessions. One particular favourite is 'Funnybones' which, using versions of the original illustrations, was not too onerous to produce.

Not all commercially produced large-format books are to be recommended, and collections of rhymes are often the best value for money. Rhyme, cumulative stories, and repetition as a meaningful part of a story (e.g. 'Hattie and the Fox') provide the kind of support which early readers, and particularly bilingual children, will need in taking on book language.

Once children have built up a repertoire of favourite stories and rhymes which have been read or told with them individually, as a class and in large versions – what is the next step? When I did finally make the break from schemes, I found that reading was much more exciting and enjoyable for everyone. Children began to talk about books more knowledgeably, and some of them made excellent progress as readers. However, I soon became aware that several children in my class who loved stories and rhymes, and had taken on language patterns to the extent of knowing several books by heart, nevertheless, while reciting these texts, looked everywhere but at the page.

These children had stayed at this stage for some

considerable time, and clearly needed help to begin to match the stories and rhymes they knew so well to the words on the page. It is important when reading with individual children at this stage to talk sometimes about features of print, to run a finger along lines of text and so on. However, classes are getting larger, and work with enlarged texts which have been previously read and enjoyed many times can support the learning in one-to-one sessions. When reading from a big book an adult can encourage the development of directionality and one-to-one correspondence by running a finger along the lines of print, or, as Don Holdaway suggests, even using a pointer to avoid masking the text with an arm. Some children never seem to find this pointing stage necessary, yet there are those for whom it is a crucial strategy for a time, as they work to make meaning and match what they know to the print on the page. Many children pass through such a stage quite naturally, and Don Holdaway quotes the example of a child lying on the floor pointing to the text of

an enlarged 'Billy Goats Gruff' with his foot!

Children can also be encouraged to look for particular features in the text, using questions such as the following

– Who can find a word on the page beginning with 'S'? With the first letter of their name?

– Can anyone find a very short word on this page? A very long word?

– Can you find a word on this page which begins with a capital letter? Why do you think it has a capital letter?

– Ask the children to look for words beginning with a particular pattern of letters e.g. 'crim, cram, crash 'em' ('Hairy Bear', Story Chest).

– Ask children whether they can find words within words.

– Are there any words which appear twice on this page?

During shared writing sessions the adult who acts as scribe can draw attention to what she is writing in similar ways. All these strategies help children to focus on print, recognise letter patterns and particular features of the way language is written, (capital letters for names, full stops etc.)

It is, however, essential that, as in Brenda Tormey's classroom, such work is part of a classroom atmosphere where there is plenty of time and encouragement for children to read and browse alone, with a friend, and to take books home, so that big book sessions do not become children's central experience of books. Children need time to reflect on books, to work on their own to make sense of a text, and to take charge of their own learning. They need the chance to practise and rehearse their reading, supported by an increasing familiarity with the stories and poetry read to them.

'Big book' sessions can be part of this process, in addition to helping children become more aware of how printed text works. Reading schemes provided the security of structure, but very often at the expense of meaningful language. To leave schemes behind is terrifying. Big books can provide support for teachers and children alike.

Gillian Lathey
Primary Advisory Teacher, London Borough of Islington

With thanks to Brenda Tormey and the children of Green Class at Hugh Myddleton Infants School.

References
Liz Waterland *Read With Me* Thimble Press, 1988 (2nd edition)
Don Holdaway *The Foundations of Literacy* Ashton Scholastic 1979

In Brenda Tormey's classroom, referred to in Gillian Lathey's article, children from the nursery sometimes join a class of top infants for their reading sessions, choosing and sharing books together. This kind of reading time cannot be called "private reading" or "silent reading" time, because many of the children choose to read together in pairs or small groups, but it is important uninterrupted time when books can be enjoyed and children can develop their ability to read independently or with the support of their peers.

Big books are an important feature of the room, both those the children have written in their "shared writing" sessions, and those that the teacher has provided for them.

OLD MOTHER HUBBARD and the GINGERBREAD MAN

Written and Illustrated by Green Class.

She had finished her curds and whey and was still hungry. So when she saw the gingerbread man she thought, "I would like to eat him". So she called out "Stop little gingerbread man, I would like to eat you!"

"No! I won't stop for you to eat me", said the gingerbread man, and he ran on and on. Then he saw Jack and Jill who were getting some water. They said "Stop little gingerbread man we want to eat you up!".

"No, I won't stop for you to eat me."

This big book is a story made up by the whole class.
"Do you remember when we wrote this book together? Which big book did we read before we wrote our own version?"
"The Enormous Watermelon"

Partners in Reading and Story-telling

Rehana Alam

I hit upon the idea suddenly one day – I even remember the month – end of September '87 with a class if 30 seven year olds at Ben Jonson School. I was getting concerned with a few children in my class who were still struggling with their reading and I was wondering how best to help them. Then – I remembered that quite a few of the giant sized 'Let's read together' books had arrived at the library the previous week. So the next day I grabbed one of the books, 'Meanies', and when all the children were assembled on the mat together, we talked about the book, the pictures, and then started reading it together. To my utter amazement and joy I found those children who always hesitated to read, read the text confidently because they were sharing the book with the others. The pattern and the rhythm seemed to have affected them emotionally and they somehow felt secure and satisfied in their own reading. From then on I made it a point to share reading with the children at least three times a day. Of course I realised that I needed to choose books which were enjoyable and meaningful to the children, not only books with beautiful pictures, but also those in which children could respond to ideas as well as feelings.

Even now when I go into different schools, I always read a giant sized 'read together book' with the whole class. The other day when I read 'Dan the Flying Man' to a class of six year olds, they came out with their own versions entitled 'Iqbal, the Flying Man'.

'I am Iqbal the flying man
Catch me, Catch me, if you can.
Over a school
Over a crane   Over the pond
Over a boat   Over trees
Over a train   Over shadows
                   Over the seas.'

Reading 'Meanies' to another class of six year olds, I was amused at how the children's imagination ran riot with their own version of what meanies ate, where they slept and so on. Connie's idea of Meanies driving coke bottles instead of baked bean tins was wonderful. When I asked little Ayesha what sort of mean things she thought Meanies did, she whispered "I don't know." "Well come on now" I urged her, "tell me in Bengali something really bad which Meanies do". Then she smiled and replied in her mother tongue "Meanies drop biscuits all over the floor!" "Well done!" I replied "That's a wonderful sentence". I noticed how her face lit up with joy when I wrote down her bit of the story in the book where we were sharing our ideas and writing our story together.

One of the most interesting experiences I had was when I read "The Cat on the Mat" to a class of 6 and 7 year olds. We read the story and there was lots of discussion about the pictures of the cat and how it got angrier and angrier when its space was taken by the other animals. This story inspired Shahana so much that she said she wanted to tell her own story and this is what she said,

"The rat sat on the mat and then the robin sat on the mat. The rat wasn't happy. The hippo came and sat next to the rat. The cow sat next to the hippo. The rat went sad. Then he said "Get off my mat – Scowww!
Then they ran away and never came back for a year and a day. Then the rat was happy"

Indeed this child was a competent reader, for she already knew that narration was made up of words and pictures together.

Bilingual kids of course, enjoy stories all the more when first told in their first language. They can immediately get involved in the story from the very start, and it becomes meaningful and pleasurable to them. The next time, when the story is repeated in English, they love it because they can predict what's coming next. Listening to the story of 'The Hungry Caterpillar' I have heard comments in Bengali and Urdu like "The Caterpillar is getting fatter and fatter, he's eaten so much" or "Ah! now comes the bit when the hungry caterpillar will turn into a beautiful butterfly."

I think the power and impact that imaginative picture books without words have on children is immense. Jomal and I were looking at 'The Snowman' book together. He rattled on excitedly in Bengali about all the adventures that took place between the little boy and the snowman just by looking at the pictures. He punctuated this at intervals with the lines "Flying in the air" sung perfectly, in English, at the most appropriate times. I spent a most entertaining fifteen minutes that day.

Learning to read and tell stories can be fun and enjoyable where both teacher and child as partners get involved in their reading in a relaxed atmosphere. I feel such relaxation creates a stress-free condition where knowledge of reading is rapidly and effortlessly absorbed by the child.

The child and teacher can become active partners in reading when they share big books together. This technique helps the child to behave like a real reader and he or she feels confident in predicting the story and recognising words and their meanings from these books. The teacher assumes the role of a guiding friend and takes over where the child cannot manage. Thereupon reading becomes a good, satisfying and meaningful experience.

Rehana Alam
Primary Induction Coordinator
Tower Hamlets

"There's them things again": shared writing and the exploration of 'linguistic awareness'

Penny Tuxford and Anne Washell

In this piece we want to look closely at the child's growing confidence in his/her ability to talk about language and the place of shared writing in this development. The kind of activity we are describing is similar to the ideas put forward in Chapter Five of the Cox Report (1988) where 'linguistic terminology' is discussed. We feel that from the beginning of their time in school children should be encouraged to find ways of talking about what they know about language and also about what they do when they use written language. A major concern for us though is to ensure that the growth of 'linguistic awareness' occurs within meaningful contexts and not in a fragmented way. We hope to show through the examples that follow, that shared writing does indeed provide a meaningful framework in which valuable discussions about language can occur.

Our interest in shared writing has been underpinned particularly by Don Holdaway's work on shared book experience as described in *The Foundations of Literacy* (1979) and also by the work of Lev Vygotsky. Both of these writers point us towards the fact that language is socially learned behaviour and this of course has implications for teaching and learning. A notion of Vygotsky's that has guided our thinking about shared writing is the 'zone of proximal development' which he describes in *Mind in Society* (1978).

> 'It is the distance between the actual development level as determined by independent problem solving and the level of potential development as determined through problem solving under adult guidance or in collaboration with more capable peers'

Our aim then, is to actively involve all children in the group or class in the shared writing session whatever their experience. We approach each session with knowledge about each child's current development as an independent writer and this informs our decisions, actions and expectations for

the individual as well as the group. Not only are we aware of the child's current needs and interests but we are ready to support him/her in moving onwards to fresh hypotheses and understandings.

In order to demonstrate the ways in which shared writing has helped us consider 'linguistic awareness' in relation to very young children we are going to look at a piece composed by a group of five and six year olds. The idea for the story *Pipsi and the Jungle* came from one of the children after the group had listened to a favourite book *The Elephant and the Bad Baby*. The other children enthusiastically supported the suggestion and so the story was written. The full text is given below in order to provide a context for what follows (the page numbers are also given):

Pipsi and the Jungle

(1) Once there was an elephant called Pipsi. She lived in a jungle.

(2) One day Pipsi was thirsty and she went to the pond to have a drink of water. She met a frog and they splashed in the water.

(3) "Ribbit, ribbit," said the frog. "See you tomorrow."

(4) Pipsi was hungry, a monkey gave Pipsi a banana. Then Pipsi gave monkey a ride.

(5) "Woo, woo, woo, woo," said the monkey "See you tomorrow."

(6) Pipsi was tired she met a hippopotamus and they went to find a place where it was cool.

(7) Pipsi and the hippopotamus fell asleep. "Good-night. See you tomorrow."

We have selected some extracts from the discussions that accompanied the composition of the piece in order to provide examples of the meaningful ways in which children gain knowledge about the writing process and how these are shared with the group as a whole. We looked in particular at three main areas: what children can do; playful discoveries that they make about words; and finally punctuation. However, as with all good stories we start at the beginning:

A Beginning

Tch: Where do I start writing? Down here?
Chn: No, up there.
Tch: Right now, what was our first sentence Joseph, can you remember what we decided?
J: Once upon a time there was a elephant called Pipsi.
Tch: (writing) Once upon a time there was an elephant called Pipsi, can anyone tell me what Pipsi begins with, what letter?
J: P
Tch: Yes good, a P, a capital P look, because it's his name
P: My name begins with P
Tch: Yes it's the same isn't it?
J: These letters in elephant (ph) are in my name.

From this initial discussion, only one sentence has been written but both the children and the teacher have opened up various opportunities for incidental learning to occur.

They have touched on how writing is laid out (i.e. where we start when we write), conventional terminology has been used (e.g. sentence and capital letter) and the use of capital letters has been explained. The teacher does not expect the children to have a real concept of capital letters or sentence at this stage, but knows that genuine

understanding grows from this and many future experiences where the terms are met in meaningful settings.

Paul's connection between his own name and Pipsi's reinforces his own knowledge of the letter 'P' and also gives the teacher an opening later on when she will ask him to come and write the first letter of Pipsi.

Joseph makes a similar connection between elephant and his name, but this time picking on two letters that commonly occur together. This kind of observation occurs frequently throughout the session and is clearly significant to the children. It would seem that it encourages them to attend to the visual aspects of spelling, such as the patterning and combination of certain letters.

A final point on the opening part of the discussion is one about grammar. The teacher automatically remodels Joseph's "a elephant" to "an elephant" when she repeats the sentence. There is no discussion about 'right' or 'wrong' but she picks up on this detail and makes sure that he hears the conventional usage.

What children can do

In shared writing sessions we have found that children are eager to put into practice what they know and can do. Joseph for example, keenly volunteered "Miss water starts with W. I can write W." By focusing on a feature that interests them or which makes appropriate links with their current knowledge they actively set up learning situations.

Sometimes the teacher seeks out less dominant members of the group to share something that she knows they can do. This occurred with Vanisha when the teacher said "Vanisha, you can write 'and' for us can't you?". Knowing about the child's current interests or capabilities enables the teacher to support the child's independent endeavours but also be there to help children do things which they cannot yet manage alone.

In the following extract, the children are

working on page 3 of the draft and are thinking out how to spell the word 'see':

Tch: Can anyone tell me how to start writing 'see'.
J: S, Miss.
E: It's like Lee

The teacher helps them to write the word but an opportunity occurs later on (at page 5) to return to the idea and reinforces successful learning strategies:

Tch: Joseph can you remember what 'see' looked like
J: Mm, not sure
Tch: Well let's have a look (turns back to page 3)
J: Oh yeah! (he turns back to the page they are writing)
Tch: Have a try (Joseph writes 'See')
J: It's like Lee.

Through their participation in shared writing children listen to and watch each other and learn collaboratively about many aspects of written language. By encouraging them to talk about what they are doing we are enabling them to realise their own knowledge.

When we support them they can achieve far more than they might on their own and as we saw in the case of Joseph above, we can begin to teach strategies for spelling which will become important in future growth.

Making Discoveries About Words

Through shared writing we have learned the importance of providing children with opportunities to talk about words. Playing with language as the Cox Report reminds us is a 'natural instinct' for children and encourages 'metalinguistic awareness'. In the following example the children explore the idea of the length of a word. They reveal their inexperience but the teacher is ready to guide them and shares her knowledge at the appropriate moment:

Tch: Do you think hippopotamus is a long word?
L: I think it's a short word.
P: So do I.
S: Long word, long word.
E: Long, yeah.
Tch. Yes I think so too.

The introduction of the idea of a 'long word' at this point was done for several reasons, but particularly to draw attention to the amount of space required to write the word 'hippopotamus'. The teacher starts to write 'Pipsi was tired she met a .....' and then asks where she should write the next word 'hippopotamus'. This provokes a lively debate by asking if she can squeeze it onto the end of a line:

J: No, there
Tch: Why?
J: 'Cos it would look funny, that's a little space
S: There isn't enough room.
P: You can't write it there.

Those three children have all articulated the same point but in slightly different ways, formulating explanations that make sense to each of them. Children need the opportunity to verbalise their feelings even if to adult ears they seem to be repeating one another. It would appear to be all part of the process of making a shared idea one's own.

The teacher then writes the word 'hippopotamus' on a new line whilst the children watch. The act of putting the word on paper sparks off a fresh area to explore concerning the length of words:

J: It's got 12 letters
E: It's longer than monkey

The children start counting the frequency of letters in words and notice recurring patterns, such as the number of times 'o' is used in the much repeated word 'woo'. They then go on to pick up

similarities between words, such as 'monkey' and 'hungry' and the idea is playfully extended to suit each child's particular needs. In the following example Joseph takes a close look at 'banana':

J: Miss in that word 'banana' (gets up and points) look it's got 3 'a's and 'n's'. It goes a-n-a-n-a (he calls out the names of the letters).
Tch: That's right it makes a pattern doesn't it? Can you see look a-n-a-n-a
J: And there's 'n' in monkey.

It is clear that children are attracted to these patterns in words and actively build hypotheses from what they know in order to make new discoveries. Shared writing provides plenty of opportunity for this to occur and each child can work at their own level as well as being exposed to the ideas of his/her more experienced peers. Words, especially the long ones or those with interesting features, hold a real fascination for children. Sacha demonstrates how even the most tenuous connections can be built upon. Her favourite word for a long time has been 'book' and she is very proud that she can spell it. Sacha likes to demonstrate this precious piece of knowledge at every opportunity and sure enough she found one:

S: Look Miss, if you take 'k' in 'monkey' and put it there (at the end of 'wood') and take that off (the 'w') and put a 'b' you get 'book'.
Tch: That's right. You do.

That Sacha felt safe to share her piece of knowledge with the group was of the utmost importance. Shared writing sessions provide a broad and flexible framework to enable this kind of thing to happen, so that all children feel that they have something worthwhile to contribute.

Punctuation
The final area that we propose to examine through this piece of shared writing is

punctuation. Young children, of course, will not have a great deal of knowledge about punctuation but through shared writing we can draw their attention to it. The foundations can be laid for future learning. This group of children looked at 'speech marks' and full stops with their teacher because they were devices that were needed during the writing of the story. The following short example shows how 'speech marks' were introduced.

Tch: Now, you've decided that frogs say "Ribbit, ribbit"... Look these (pointing to the speech marks) are like we saw in *The Elephant and the Bad Baby*. Can you remember? We put them round things that people say. We call them speech marks.

Later on when speech marks were needed again, Paul commented:

P: There's them things again.

It is in this way, by acknowledging the presence of punctuation as Paul does here, that children begin to become aware of its functions and find ways of talking about it.

As we have shown, we want all children to feel they have something worthwhile to contribute to a shared writing session whether it be in supplying ideas for the content of the story or making observations of the kind described above. With some children we may well be satisfied to see them closely observing the text that is being created and listening to the discussion. Shared writing through its demonstrations is especially useful for children such as these. In each session we aim for a balance content and surface features but most of all we want children to enjoy and show enthusiasm for it.

We think that through shared writing children will meet many of the aspects of writing highlighted in the Cox Report and see it as particularly useful when introducing children to 'linguistic terminology'. Shared writing sessions

give us the opportunity to make knowledge about language explicit but always within meaningful situations. There is no need for children to meet terms such as 'adjective' or 'speech marks' out of context. Shared writing ensures that this knowledge is gained in appropriate ways and also enables children to meet the same notions many times over but always in a memorable way. Because children are actively involved, and their current knowledge and understandings are valued, they are enabled to take their first steps in learning how to talk about language.

In this article we have focused on metalinguistic matters but it may be necessary to point out that shared writing is not just an occasion for talking about language. The main focus always needs to be on the developing text itself. Above all, when we write with children, we are concerned with meaning.

To conclude, we return to Vygotsky with whom we find ourselves in complete agreement when he says:

...what a child can do with assistance today she will be able to do by herself tomorrow.

Surely, through the supportive and secure experience of shared writing children are helped by their teacher and peers to move towards genuine independence in their written language. If we can see this happen, in even the smallest way, then we should be well satisfied.

Penny Tuxford and Anne Washtell
Wix School

References
English for ages 5 to 11 (The Cox Report) DES, November 1988
Don Holdaway, *The Foundations of Literacy* Ashton Scholastic 1979
Lev Vygotsky, *Mind in Society: The Development of Higher Psychological Processes* Harvard, 1978
Raymond Briggs and Elfrida Vipont *The Elephant and the Bad Baby* Picture Puffins

Mrs Wishy Washy has become a favourite text in this reception infants class. The big book version of the story is constantly in use, and children are playing at being Mrs Wishy Washy in the home corner. Their teacher, Penny Tuxford, thinks that one of the attractions of the book is the name of the main character, Mrs Wishy Washy; the children enjoy the play of sounds in the words. This week they decide to do their own Mrs Wishy Washy book. It is their first really extended piece of shared writing.

Before they start to write on this particular occasion the class reads "the story so far" together. This enables them to revisit a text they have made, recognising and beginning to read the words on the page, and hearing the tune of the story they are making.

Penny has a way of "wondering aloud" which encourages the children to think about the situation they are creating. "*I wonder what she did? I wonder who it was from? I wonder what the zoo would be asking Mrs Wishy Washy to do? I wonder what it will say on the next page?*".

Any text in "shared writing" is a compromise. Children offer different possibilities, and somehow a final text emerges. The words underlined in the following transcription of the discussion are those that eventually become the text on the page:

"Mrs Wishy Washy – <u>read the letter</u> – picked it up – opened it – <u>read the letter</u> – and she laughed – and she said – and it said – "Mrs Wishy Washy, please could you wash our animals tomorrow?" – and she laughed – Ha ha ha – (*Do you want that writing?*) – "<u>Ha ha ha ha ha</u>".

"*I wonder what the letter said? What do you think the letter was asking? Who was it from?*"
"<u>The</u> postman – the postman brought it – from the Zoo"
"*What do you think the Zoo was asking?*"
"Please can you wash our animals?"
"*If we say 'Please can you wash our animals' it might sound as if Mrs Wishy Washy was saying it. Do you want to put 'It said' or 'The letter said'?*"
"<u>The letter said 'Please could you wash</u> our animals –"
"*Our animals?*"
"– <u>the animals</u>"
"*Where?*"
"– <u>in the Zoo</u>."

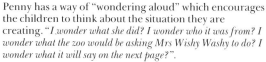
17

Shared Writing-'People Working Together'

Liz Laycock

"Especially when writing is being learned, there is often a great need for and advantage in people working together on a letter, a poem or a story. The ability to write alone comes with experience and is not always easy or necessary."
Frank Smith

There are as many contexts for 'working together' or shared writing as there are purposes for writing. Any kind of writing, other than the most personal, can be undertaken in collaboration with others. The 'people working together' may be two or three friends, a larger group of children, an individual child working with an adult or a group of children working with a teacher. Any of these groupings could be writing a list (e.g. of questions to ask a visitor to the classroom), an account of an experience they have shared (e.g. a visit), instructions for doing or making something (e.g. how to make a working model), a poem, a letter or a story. Such collaboration allows the creation of texts which could not have been achieved by individual children working alone: for some children they may be the only texts which enable them to experience the satisfaction which comes from composing a complete story or poem or letter.

Writing shared between an individual child and an adult, especially at the earliest stages when the child does not have control of the transcriptional skills needed to record what s/he wishes to say, separates what Smith (1982) terms 'composition' of the text (i.e. the ideas, the selection of words and the grammar) from its 'transcription' (i.e. the physical effort, the spelling, the punctuation etc.). Smith speaks of the continual conflict for any individual writer between these two aspects of writing: "Composition and transcription can interfere with each other. The more attention you give to one, the more the other is likely to suffer." The two, he believes, must be separated; in shared

writing there is generally a physical separation.

The five year old who composed this text (below) could not have transcribed it himself, but collaboration with a teacher allowed the creation of a long story and allowed him to experience the satisfaction of being a writer:–

A Funny Book (Boy, age 5.1)

'A man was walking on the street and he saw a door and he opened the door and some big, fat pigs were in the room. The man who was walking on the street went through the door and he saw the big, fat pigs and he saw a chair. He sat on the chair and the chair fell down and he fell in the bath and the big fat pigs pulled him out. And the roof fell down and

the man who was walking in the street fell back in the bath again. He climbed out again and did a funny dance to shake all the water off. And then the big fat pigs tried to frighten the man. They climbed up lamp posts to frighten the man and they jumped out of dust bins to frighten the man, and then the man crawled out of the door just like a baby. He crawled all the way home calling, 'Help, help, help, help, help, help, help, help, help.' He opened the door of his house, he shut it again and then it got stuck and he had to eat it. And then he went in the house and went to bed because he was tired of crawling all the way home. And before he went to bed he washed his clothes.'

Detectable here are direct influences from stories he is familiar with ("Funny Bones" – J and A Ahlberg) as well as his knowledge of narrative structure, a real appreciation of literary language and of the rhythms of written language. None of this would have been revealed without the opportunity to collaborate, to work as an apprentice alongside a more experienced scribe.

Similar divisions of labour can be seen in shared writing undertaken by pairs or groups of children, working without a teacher. In these situations the young writers often take it in turns to write down what they want to say, with the result that the physical effort does not become overpowering and ideas are generated through discussion. Often, the child who is not transcribing will initiate a new idea, reflect upon it and develop the story, as the two girls do in this extract from a longer composition session. Jade is writing down the story at this point:–

Jade: Went back
Rita: to the bedroom, what else
Jade: back to the bedroom, bedroom... and got
Rita: "Opened her wardrobe and started to choose some clothes to wear to, for that day", go on
Jade: "and got dressed specially for that day"
Rita: Yeh go on then
Jade: got dressed specially, got specially dressed
Rita: No got dressed especially
Jade: dressed spe – em, special for that
Rita: "for that day as she was going to meet the government", no what. What's she meet? (takes paper)
Yes, the government (slaps it back wrong side up).

Within a larger group there is even more space for reflection on the ideas or events, for evaluation of the effect of the words chosen. If one group member suggests a sentence, an event, or a way of expressing something, others in the group will assess the effectiveness of that suggestion and

changes or modifications may be incorporated. A group of five year olds, working with their teacher, composing a story about a girl climbing a beanstalk, agreed they wanted to say:

> ".... she tried to climb up the beanstalk (A), holding onto the (B) leaves tightly...."

One boy in the group suggested adding "slowly, slowly" after "beanstalk" (A) because it "told you how hard it was to climb"; he also added "golden" before "leaves" (B) because, earlier in the story, the group had said that the leaves were gold.

Shared writing can focus not only on the effectiveness of words but also on the enjoyment to be had from playing with words. Often we concentrate our teaching on the serious aspects of both composition and transcription and do not capitalise on the pleasure children find in the sound of language or on their love of nonsense. Play with the sound of language begins very early in a child's development. Ruth Weir (1962) recorded her son, Anthony's, pre-sleep monologues: he seems often to explore the rhymes and rhythms of language for their own sake, not because they are intended to communicate meaning:–

Bink,
Let Bobo bink,
Bing ben bink,
Blue kink.
(Anthony 2.5)

Older children will frequently invent nonsense rhymes:–

Once upon a ping pong,
There was a little jing-jong,
Sitting on a ding-dong,
Eating up his fing-fong,
He was a bong-bong.
(Boy 5.6)

In this the child is clearly "enjoying the sounds and the act of articulating" (Holdaway 1979).

One group of children – eight first year juniors – inspired by Jonathan Coudrille's sophisticated alphabet book, 'A Beastly Collection', which plays with both sound, words, meanings and with visual interpretation of ideas, worked with great enthusiasm and concentration to produce their own crazy alphabet. This collaboration included the teacher initially, who wrote down their first silly story as they composed – 'Tony the Tyrannosaurus tripped over Tommy the Tiger, then tossed Tracy the Turtle into the teapot...' Later collaborations between pairs and groups of children without the teacher produced others about 'Alonzo the awful Alligator always eating apples....', about 'Brian the busy Bear baking bread' with 'Buzzy Bee buzzing below busy Bear's beautiful bottom and biting bits of busy Bear's bread....', and about 'Cuthbert the clever cooking Cat' who 'couldn't cook a chocolate cake....'

Frequently the demonstration, through shared writing with the teacher, of a particular kind of writing, brings about not only imitation but reflection upon the way a particular kind of text is constructed and about the characteristics of a particular genre. In order to be able to create their own texts in a particular form, young writers need to have heard or read examples of that genre. Much of what they need to know they will acquire

unconsciously, but discussion and group creation of texts in a particular genre may make their knowledge explicit, enable children to articulate their understandings and allow them to experiment with a familiar form by incorporating variations.

The group of five year olds referred to earlier had heard both the traditional tale of 'Jack and the Beanstalk' and Raymond Briggs' 'Jim and the Beanstalk' before they composed their own 'Michaela and the Beanstalk'. The choice of a girl for the hero was the result of a long discussion and a vote before they began to compose. Their story was written down by the teacher over many short sessions – about twenty minutes each – when, sometimes, they simply re-read and discussed what had already been written without adding more:–

'Once upon a time Michaela looked out of the window and she saw an enormous (1), plant. She got dressed and she sneaked out of the house. She looked around her and she was very surprised to see the beanstalk had golden (2) leaves. It was one hundred feet high and it touched the sky. Michaela felt scared. Even if she was scared (3), she thought she would climb up it. She tried to climb up the beanstalk slowly, slowly holding onto the golden leaves tightly.

She climbed and climbed until she got to the top. Michaela saw a great big castle. "I hope they have cornflakes," she said to herself. She knocked on the door but (everything was silent) in the castle. The giant's (nobody was – deleted) brother was sleeping in the castle. He woke up and stamped (4), to the door and he said in a loud voice, "Fee Fi Fo Fum, I smell

the blood of an Englishman, Be he alive or be he dead, I'll grind his bones to make my bread." Michaela was trembling when she heard the giant's brother's voice. "What do you want for breakfast?" said the giant's brother. "Can I have some cornflakes, please, and some milk?" said Michaela. When she finished her cornflakes she said, "Thankyou and goodbye!" And the giant said, "Goodbye, you can come to my house anytime you like."

The sun was so hot that it melted the golden leaves and she slipped down the beanstalk. She told her mummy all about her adventures but her mum didn't believe a word (6).'

We see the obvious features of the fairy story genre – a conventional opening and some typical comments, 'an enormous plant' (1), with 'golden leaves' (2), appearing by magic, the 'scared' hero (3), overcoming fear, a 'stamping' (4) giant using the traditional 'Fee Fi Fo' rhyme, a happy ending. There are also variations – the realistic breakfast, the politeness (5), of both the hero and the giant, the sceptical mother (6), and the conflict necessary in a fairy story is missing. These children could neither have composed at this length alone, nor increased their knowledge of this particular genre outside the collaborative shared writing context.

A group of older children (seven first year juniors) also worked on the fairy story genre. They had read Tony Ross's version of 'Puss in Boots', in which the hero's two brothers, lazy Harry and Good-For-Nothing Tom. are introduced at the beginning and then do not appear again.

These children decided to write the story of one of the brothers, Good-For-Nothing Tom, who inherits a horse in the Miller's will, just as Jack inherits Puss. Their story was composed over three long sessions. At the end of the second they and the teacher with whom they worked thought the story was finished, but re-reading at the third session led to major revisions.

Good-For-Nothing Tom and his Horse, Sandy

Once upon a time there was an old man [a miller] (1) who had three sons. He was very old and ill and one day he died. Just before he died he called his sone and said. "Before I die I will give each of you, Harry, Tom and Jack, a gift. Harry, you will have the mill and my grandfather clock"

"Thanks, dad," said Harry, but he was too lazy to say anything else.

"Jack, you can have the cat and my bookrack."

"Thanks very much dad," said Jack. "Yippee" That's great, I love the cat – he's soft and furry."

"Tom, you can have the horse and my big sack and little bit of my gold money."

[Tom said "Thanks very much, dad, you are really kind. I love you, dad, I hope you don't die."] (2)

The old man died that night. Next morning Tom found he was dead. He ran away crying, he got the horse and the gold and galloped off to the inn. He spent (3) [several pieces of gold] ~~one piece of gold~~ on beer and got drunk. After a long time he called "Sandy, come eer..eer" The horse galloped to him and Tom climbed on. They speeded off into the woods. While he was on the horse he couldn't see very well – his head was full of stars and his eyes got more and

more drowsy. He went to sleep and flopped over the horse's head. Sandy walked on and on until they were lost.

Late in the night when Tom and Sandy were both feeling sleepy, they suddenly fell down, down, down into a trap. They were in great danger. The bump when they landed woke them up.

But this horse [Sandy] (4) was not scared. He said "Don't fear, Tom. I will save you by flying." Slowly her sides began to grow wider and a pair of furry soft wings began to grow. "Tom", she called, "wake up. Climb onto my back and we won't be trapped here for long". Sandy spread out her wings and swooped up out of the pit. They flew off into the sky and as they flew out the pit started to collapse.

They flew a long way and a long time. Her wings got tired and Sandy saw a castle.

When she got closer they could hear gun shots and a spear came flying up and just missed them. They looked down and saw a great crowd of guards fighting an army. They were trying to get into the castle to kidnap the Princess Mary. Sandy the horse said, "Tom, we need to help them fight". They swooped down and Tom found he'd got a sword and a shield in his hands. For an hour they fought with the King's guard and they won the battle.

(5) [Tom and Sandy were fighting the army. Tom whizzed the sword around and [slashed] ~~cut off~~

some soldiers heads. Blood was pouring everywhere. Sandy charged and kicked the soldiers out of the way and trod on them. At the end all the [enemies] ~~soldiers~~ were dead. The princess was crying to see so many poor people killed.]

The king was so glad he said, (6) ["What is your name, my son?" "My name is Tom, your Majesty"] "You brave man, you can marry my daughter, Princess Mary"

(7) [Tom said to Princess Mary, "Will you marry me?" She said, "No, not until I know you a bit better." For the next ten days they talked together, they ate great big feasts, they danced with each other at big parties, they went riding and flying on the magic horse, Sandy, to have a holiday in Athens in Greece. They swam in the sea and looked at the beautiful [buildings] ~~places~~ .(8) While they were away the King [and the guards] (9) buried all the dead soldiers in a special grave-yard. When Princess Mary and Tom came back they decided to get married. So they got married and lived in the castle. Guess who lived in the next castle? Jack and his clever cat.

(10) [If you want to know who Jack is, read the story of 'Puss in Boots'.]

N.B. Alterations and additions are shown thus;
[Enclosed in square brackets = additions]
Dotted underlinings e.g. = deletions.

Without a direct transcription of the discussion which took place in this final revision, it is possible only to indicate the variety of the children's concerns:–

1. The children felt it was necessary to add 'a miller' because Harry inherited the mill and it should be explained.

2. One member of the group noticed that the other brothers had been made to say thank you and thought Tom should. She also wanted him, because he was the hero of the story, to say something kind to the miller.

3. This addition was the result of the discussion about whether it was possible to buy enough beer to get drunk with just 'one piece of gold'!

5. This long section was added because one boy said it sounded as though Tom and Sandy were fighting against the king's guard and 'there ought to be more about the fight'. The description of the fight owes more, perhaps, to the comic-book/ super-hero genre or even myth and legend, than it does to the fairy story, but for these children it may be that the unrealistic elements of all of these are interchangeable.

6/7. In the fairy story the hero battles with evil and is rewarded by marriage to a princess. The children wanted to be true to the genre they were writing in, but another boy said he thought the king ought to ask Tom's name before he offered the princess. It was a girl who thought that Tom should, at least, ask the princess to marry him and that she ought to find out something about him before she agreed to do so. It was never in doubt that they would marry and 'live happily ever after' but, perhaps because of encounters with more modern fairy stories ('The Paper Bag Princess', 'The Clever Princess' and 'The Practical Princess') the children agreed that she need not simply accept immediately.

8. The suggestion that Tom and the Princess travel to Greece came from a girl of Greek origin, who drew upon her direct experience of Athens to define more closely what, in her view, was important about that city – the buildings.

9. Some discussion about what had happened to all the bodies led to their burial in 'a special graveyard' and further discussion about whether kings did things like digging graves brought about the addition of 'and the guards'.

10. This last sentence was included because the group wanted to make sure their readers would know who 'Jack and his clever cat' were. In this, as in other changes, they showed a real awareness of the needs of the reader.

These refinements to the story the seven children had created would almost certainly, not have been made if any one of them had written this fairy tale alone. The collaboration and their discussion refined not only the story but also their own understanding of the elements which must be present; together they were able to maintain the appropriate style and make explicit their knowledge of the genre.

It must be said that at seven or eight years of age many children already have a fairly secure grasp of this particular narrative form and that they find other kinds of writing more difficult. Kress (1982) states that 'the child has to gain mastery over the forms and the possibilities of the different generic types as part of the process of learning to write... But if the teaching of writing has received little attention, the teaching of genre has had even less...' Whilst poetry, different forms of narrative, letters and humorous writing are often undertaken collaboratively, factual, scientific, 'transactional' writing is more often produced by children working alone. But collaboration between more experienced (generally adult) and less experienced writers of factual accounts could help to make explicit the requirements of these forms too. If sharing the writing of stories provides a useful learning context it should be possible to extend the variety of writing undertaken in this way, to include factual and scientific accounts. This would allow discussion about the structure and organisation of such texts as well as about the appropriateness of vocabulary used and the effectiveness of the communication. Collaboration on many different levels is an important part of a full writing experience in the classroom. Provision needs to be made for this as well as for children to write individually and for more personal purposes.

Liz Laycock

References

Don Holdaway *'The Foundations of Literacy'* (1979)
Gunther Kress *'Learning to Write'* (1982)
Frank Smith *'Writing and the Writer'* (1982)
Ruth Weir *'Language in the Crib'* (1962)
Jonathan Coudrille *'A Beastly Collection'*
J. & A. Ahlberg *'Funny Bones'*
Raymond Briggs *'Jim and the Beanstalk'*
Tony Ross *'Puss in Boots'*
Robert Munsch *'The Paper-bag Princess'*
Diana Coles *'The Clever Princess'*
Jay Williams *'The Practical Princess'*

Over the Wall: a shared experience

Audrey Ringrose

Shared writing is potentially an effective and economical means of teaching young children the art of story writing. All the skills can be practised: the handling of narrative, dialogue and description, the development of character and plot, the evocation of an intended response in a reader. Group discussion of the best way to bring about an effect, the most telling word to use, how a character might behave, can be the beginnings of literary criticsm. Later, when the mechanics of writing are established, this critical skill learned in a group situation, can lead to children's independent appraisal of their own stories. Additionally, if the writing is continued over several weeks by alternating groups, reading the previous instalments in order to continue the narrative requires a high level of comprehension.

But – and the 'but' is a big one – these skills can only be learned by the children who most need them, if the interest of the whole group is maintained during the writing session. Only too often what passes as a shared story is actually the work of a handful of articulate and assertive children. The rest have scuffled around the fringes of the group, bickering more or less quietly and paying frequent visits to the toilet. Even worse, some may have sat smiling blandly, totally untouched by the proceedings. A teacher's diplomatic skills will only go so far to engage and maintain the interest of every child in the group. After that, it could be switch-off time for the majority.

I think the crucial decision lies in the choice of subject matter. What are you going to make the story out of? Nothing will come of nothing. Young children are by definition short on experience, yet experience is the raw material of creative writing. What we need is experience of such cogency that children want to put it into a story. And if it is to be a shared story, then the experience must be shared also.

Reading to the class is a beginning, and I have found that if I help children to actualise the fiction by creating an appropriate setting, by drama, role play and discussion, by an imaginative use of the environment, and by linking the story to their own lives, children transform the fiction and it becomes a real part of their own experience.

This happened with the shared writing of 'The Iron Man', which I have written about elsewhere. As far as possible I had put the children through the same experiences the Iron Man has in Ted Hughes' tale, so that they had lived the story long before we started writing our own version.

In the story I am concerned with here, the children were even more deeply involved. Not only did they experience the events they later recorded, but, to an important extent, they were responsible for what happened.

Let's go back to the beginning, a whole term before the writing started. It was November. I was in despair. Christmas was looming with its inevitable concomitant – the Christmas show. I had a particularly idiosyncratic class of thirty middle infants. Their characteristic behaviour was like mercury liberated from the thermometer. Volatile and unpredictable, their liaisons were ephemeral in the extreme. The prospect of uniting them into a cohesive group in order to present them in public was daunting. Straight-jackets were out of the question. Too expensive.

I was fortunate in having Linda, a multi-talented support teacher, working with me for two days a week. She advised me to write a narrative which she and I would read and which the class could respond to with music, mime, dance and their own dialogue. In this way, their confines would be clear but there would be plenty of participation for them. Linda outlined a situation we might start from: two countries, one fertile and prosperous, the other impoverished. The people of the rich land won't share with the poor people. Some disaster occurs in which the positions are reversed, and the class would be left to resolve the ending.

I could see the practical possibilities of her idea, and also hoped that we might slip in some moral and social education on the way. So I went away and wrote 'The Wall', stopping the narrative when I got to the crisis, and we went into rehearsal.

From the beginning we worked with scenery. This consisted of one bench dividing the acting area to represent the wall. We also added two parallel benches to which the children retired when they were not performing.

R E T I R I N G	ACTING	T H E	ACTING	R E T I R I N G
	AREA		AREA	
	GREENLAND	W A L L	GREYLAND	
B E N C H				B E N C H

Six children became musicians who were to devise sound effects; of the rest, twelve became Greenlanders and twelve were Greylanders.

The play opened with the two groups on stage facing away from each other separated by the bench. The Greenlanders sprawled in the sunshine, the Greylanders crouched in defensive huddles:

> "Once upon a time in another world there were two countries. One was called Greenland and the other was called Greyland. Although the countries were next to each other, they were separated by a high brick wall."

Then the Greylanders retired to their bench while the Greenlanders mimed to the narration:

"Now Greenland was a fertile country. The sun shone cheerfully, the wind blew gently and the rain fell kindly. Trees in the forest grew tall and proud and the people used the trunks to build themselves houses, and at night they sat round fires made from the branches. Delicious fruit hung in the orchards, wheat grew in the fields, cows oozing with milk feasted in the green meadows. The hens laid so many eggs that the children used them as ping-pong balls. The people of Greenland grew tall and strong and proud like their forests. At night they danced round their fires".

Linda taught the Greenlanders to respond

sensitively to the sun, wind and rain; they mimed cutting down trees, hauling logs and building houses. They built a fire, stuffed themselves with juicy fruit and batted ping-pong eggs at each other. They improvised a rollicking dance round the fire. The musicians selected instruments to illustrate their carefree way of life.

Now it was the turn of the Greylanders to take the stage:

"But next door in Greyland it was very different. The earth was rocky and barren. When the sun shone, it blazed without mercy; when the wind blew, it howled like a demon; when the rain fell it fell like nails. Trees could not grow in the barren earth, so the people crept under prickly bushes for shelter. They ate bitter berries from the thorny bushes and their only drink was water from the stony streams. The Greyland people were small and shrivelled and bony, like the very bushes they lived under, and their dance was weary".

The Greylanders cringed under the onslaught of the rain and wind. They twisted their bodies into distorted shapes as they crept over the stony ground to scoop up water and pick berries; they limped painfully in a travesty of dancing.

Then came the confrontation:

"One day, the Greyland people found out about Greenland, and it happened like this. A child clambered oh so painfully, oh so slowly, up a high stony rock and looked over the high brick wall into Greenland. She called "Come and look at this everybody." All the Greyland people climbed oh so painfully, oh so slowly, up the high stony rock and looked at the wonderful country over the wall."

The children described what they could see over the wall, some drawing on the narration, some on imagination, and their improvised dialogue was incorporated in the text:

"Look! Lots of trees with fruit.
And lovely daffodils.
And houses.
A beautiful sky with birds in it.
And chickens.
And cows and pigs.
And strong people.
And strong trees.
They all called to the Greenland people; Oh please can we come over the wall?"

Then came everyone's favourite piece of action:

"But the Greenland people put out their tongues, folded their arms, stamped their feet and turned their backs. And their leader shouted: Go away. You're spoiling our view!"

Both groups devised songs, set to short passages of music from Vivaldi's "Four Seasons" which were used at this point to illustrate the stalemate:

"Freezing, shivering, starving, rumbling, sad . . .
Bony, stony, lonely, prickly, sad . .".

was the Greyland song in a minor key. The Greenland song went like this:

"We are happy,
Food is lovely,
We eat juicy fruit.
We cut trees down
With our axes,
We make houses warm."

Next came the disaster:

"Then one night something really dreadful happened. The people of Greenland were tucked up in their snug houses, when a hurricane came roaring out of nowhere. A great block-buster of a wind! It tore trees up out of the ground and threw them into the air. It blew down houses as if they were matchboxes. The hens and even the cows went riding on the back of that great wind. Torrential rain fell in buckets and beat out the fires and flooded the meadows.

In Greyland, the people cowered under the low prickly bushes and listened fearfully as the wild hurricane passed over their heads."

This part of the narrative gave opportunities for almost unbridled movement and mime from the Greenlanders and led to an unleashing of sound effects from the percussionists. It was 1987, the year of the hurricane which had made a vivid impression on the children, so they were able to draw on personal experience for this scene.

After the disaster the situations were reversed:

"When the hurricane had gone, the Greylanders dared to creep out and what did they find? Their dry land was watered, seeds had blown over the wall and started to sprout. And the hurricane had even dropped some cows and chickens. Now Greyland became the fertile country where the sun shone cheerfully, the wind blew gently and the rain fell kindly."

The Greylanders wallowed in mud, watched

seedlings grow into young trees, cradled chickens and patted cows. Their land blossomed and they grew proud and strong and sang the complacent song.

Greenland was left with nothing:

"The people were shrivelling up like dried leaves."

and they sang the dreary song.

When the Greenlanders found out that all their luck was on the other side of the wall, it was their turn to plead to come over.

At this point I had stopped the narrative and left the class to resolve the problem. First of all, I found that it was imperative for the Greylanders to put out their tongues, fold their arms, stamp their feet and turn their backs and for their leader to shout "Go away! You're spoiling our view!" After that they were quite willing to enter into a discussion.

I call it a discussion, but that's a polite term for what followed. The Greylanders were adamant that the Greenlanders should not come over the wall. So it was up to the Greenlanders to persuade them. A slanging match developed: only the presence of the wall prevented fisticuffs. My private hopes of fostering moral development dwindled.

Then Ellie, a very forceful Greylander, said: "It's like Ethiopia – we help Ethiopia, why shouldn't we help Greenland? We've got enough for them to share." A furious argument began among the Greylanders. I held my breath. But Ellie, by persuasion and coercion, gradually got her way. The argument was distilled into the following dialogue:

"Don't be so mean! Why can't they come over?

Because they didn't let us come over when we asked.

Yes! That's right!

Remember how we felt when it was us? I agree with Ellie.

Why can't they share our land with us?

Can we trust them?

We promise to be good.

We'll help you build houses.

Yes, we'll all be friends."

The final coup de théâtre was to swing round the bench representing the wall and turn it into a bridge between the two countries. There the company assembled for a final song extolling the virtues of sharing and co-operation.

Once the production had taken shape, we would finish rehearsals with a discussion of the issues. It was a revelation to find that, when the drama had stopped, most Greylanders reverted to their original impulse to keep out the Greenlanders. In fact David, another forceful Greylander, was apoplectic with fury. "It's not a true end," he raged, "I said they couldn't come over because they didn't let us come over and then you let them come over." And he did, in fact, exchange blows with Ellie, whom he felt to be a traitor to her side.

What we had done was to cut down the internecine strife in the class and instead produced two passionately opposed factions. So much for our well-meaning social engineering.

But we were not done with tinkering yet. Over the Christmas holidays we hatched our plans....

In the Spring term, Linda started work on a model of Greyland and Greenland. Everyone in the class worked on both sides of the wall. They made frequent references to the play text and dug back into their memories to recall what they had added. They used the environment as copy – the infant log cabin, trees, bushes, themselves.

At the same time, I began work on the shared story, working with half the class at a time and making sure that everyone crossed the wall and had the opportunity to write from a different point of view.

This time there was no question of non-involvement. Everyone clamoured to contribute and the problem was to avoid disappointment and hurt feelings. Discussions had to be conducted with the utmost diplomacy. The shared experience provided the materiál. The model-making was a new aspect which was fertilising the original form and keeping it alive.

The argument was never about what should happen next, but rather about the best way of presenting it. I was gratified to find that one of my secret intentions had succeeded. I had deliberately written the narrative in a 'literary' style and this I found the children had not only assimilated, but were now making successful variations of their own. For example, look at the opening sentence of their version.

> Years ago, in another world, there was an old wall standing there silently. It was very tall, crumbly, hard, cracky and scratchy. The sun shone on one side of the wall to make it warm. The warm side was Greenland.

Sometimes they quoted chunks of the original:

> But the Greenland people stuck out their tongues, stamped their feet, folded their arms and turned their backs. And their leader said, "Go away! You're spoiling our view."

But more often they embellished my narrative with memories of what they had actually done in the play:

> Greenland had a lot of trees with juicy fruit on. When the people ate the fruit, the juice dribbled down their chins. They chopped down the gigantic trees with their sharp, mighty axes to build houses. At night, they danced round their blazing fire.

This concrete and detailed description of the view over the wall was what they had visualised in the play. And notice how they changed the direct speech into narrative with, as far as I recall, utmost confidence:

> One day a child climbed over the sharp rocks and looked over the wall into Greenland. She saw cows, hens, strong people, tall trees with fruit, houses, daffodils and a beautiful sky with birds in it.

You can see in the following passage how they use my similes as stepping stones to step on to their own:

> The other side of the wall was Greyland. The rain fell down like nails, the wind howled like a demon, the sun shone without mercy. The Greyland people curled up under the prickly bushes like caterpillars.

When they came to describe the night of the hurricane, there was a marvelous fusion of my narrative, their mime and music, imagination and, of course, personal memories of the October hurricane:

> Suddenly there was a loud clap of thunder. Crash went the windows! Swoosh went the wind down the chimneys and blew out the fires. Trees were uprooted. Cows and hens were blown over the wall. It was a hurricane! The Greenland people screamed and cried and were tossed up in the air in circles like pancakes. They were dizzy!

> The Greyland people were hiding under the prickly bushes. They heard water bubbling and wish-washing in the stony stream, the rain flattened their hair, they saw flying cows, pigs, people and chickens flapping their wings and squawking like murder. They saw dark clouds flying past and heard crashing claps of thunder.

I think this was the most satisfying shared story I'd ever embarked on. The writing was done over a period of about six weeks and because the content was so firmly established beforehand, we were able to focus on matters of style. The children expanded their descriptive powers and showed an intuitive understanding of how to modulate the narrative in order to bring about a desired response in a reader. Their opening sentence is a particularly good example of this: "Years ago, in another world, there was an old wall standing there silently." Straightaway, the focus is on that wall; the phrase "standing there silently" imbues it with significance. A reader knows instinctively that the wall is to be crucial in the story.

The success of this story was entirely dependent on the preceding experience that provided the raw material. I don't know that I made any appreciable impact on the moral education of the class as a whole. Still, some children were roused to take up the cause of the under-privileged. You can't really expect this of all six-year olds. I do know that the class enjoyed doing the play and writing the story. They loved reading "The Wall" for themselves, but even more they loved having it read to them. In fact, when an unwary teacher went in at story-time and read it to them, she came out white and shaken. "Is that what they call audience participation?" she whispered weakly.

Audrey Ringrose

Reference
Audrey Ringrose *Language Matters Nos. 2 & 3, 1987* "From Sharing to Independence"

Shared Writing and Poetry with Top Juniors
Helen Kerslake

Shared writing as a technique for working together, with teacher as scribe, helping draw children's attention to print, is used extensively with young children and has been frequently written about. However – for top juniors? Comments I've heard include 'it's just a more intimate use of the blackboard' or 'Perhaps useful for those children who are still beginners but most top juniors should be writing independently.'

When many infant teachers were reclaiming old painting easels and children-sized blackboards from old store rooms for their newly discovered 'shared writing', I was teaching top juniors and eager to try some myself. I quickly discovered its value and versatility for older children and have been using it ever since with my own classes and others I've worked with.

As a technique you can use it for helping children to learn about both the transcriptive aspects of writing – spelling, language conventions (e.g. speech marks, handwriting) and the compositional aspects; focusing more on one than the other on different occasions depending on what you want children to learn. It's versatility and the possibility of its use with both small and large groups of children make it a very powerful teaching technique.

Shared Writing – Focusing on Transcription

I believe that if all the children you are working with can see what you're writing and are encouraged to read it then they will almost inevitably be taking in something about the transcription aspects of the writing at their own level. Yet you can use shared writing in other more systematic and planned ways by deliberately drawing children's attention to the spelling of particular words. For example 'masking' words and getting children to remember them, drawing attention to word patterns, words within words, are not just activities more suited for younger

children. You can also look at clever plays on words, rhymes, alliteration and so on.

From time to time you may want to focus on something that has been coming up as an issue in some of your children's own writing. A group who are persistently over-using apostrophes, for example, could be brought together for a quick shared writing session. Of course you may want to introduce or remind children about something with the whole class when you are all together.

Shared writing can also be a very good way of drawing children's attention to handwriting. You can talk about the style you are using, and on occasions you can slow down, take care, and show ways of joining letters together in the school's style.

Shared Writing – Focusing on Composition

Although the scope is limitless, on the whole with older children, I've used shared writing for composing with the whole class, or large groups of children (10-15), and predominantly for four different types of writing.

1. *Non-fiction*

This has frequently been the starting-point for introducing a new class project, involving a gathering of everything we already knew about a given project/topic. This information has been turned into a non-fiction book for the classroom by a group of children. A preliminary sharing session has sometimes been followed by a session where we pose questions to try and answer later or decide on areas of interest to find out more about. (Part of this shared writing sometimes took the form of a topic web or flow chart.)

2. *Narrative Writing*

I always like to give children opportunities to write their own stories about anything they choose. However I realise that getting children to think

carefully about the structure of their own story writing and develop awareness of an audience involves help and intervention. I have always found it enormously useful to plan a complete story with a group of children or the whole class. This would perhaps involve thinking about an exciting beginning to get readers quickly interested, a carefully thought out middle, with plot developments that ensure all threads are 'picked up', and of course a decent ending that reveals all and preferably ties up any loose ends. I had always done this orally, but then discovered that scribing plans for stories on large sheets of kitchen paper proved more rewarding and purposeful. It gave a much more focused feel to the task, and provided a nice illustration of rough initial planning for children. It demonstrated that changing one's mind and crossing out, making additions and abandoning ideas later, were all part of the process.

After completing one of these plans I have even written extended stories with my whole class as a shared writing activity. However, I found sustaining interest and maintaining all the threads of a complicated story with a whole class over a long period of time pretty hard going. A more successful project was to plan and begin a story together and then break it into sections for pairs of children to work on, before assembling it, finishing it off together, and finally editing it.

3. *Poetry*

A poem is obviously a much more managable shared writing task than a story and I have written a lot of poetry with juniors in this way which I mean to discuss in more detail later in this article.

4. *Letters, notes, messages etc.*

This is the more usual means of using shared writing with older juniors and is traditionally done on the blackboard. A quick collaborative effort to write something that, hopefully, everyone can agree on for a clear purpose, (e.g. a get well card, a letter to a local factory asking to visit, something to be read out in assembly and so on). Sometimes this process will model a particular form of writing e.g. letter writing.

Answering teachers' concerns

Some teachers have expressed the following reservations about shared writing with older children.

> "Who's the author? Who has ownership of a piece of shared writing?"

I don't view this as a problem if you see it very much as a corporate enterprise, belonging to everybody, the task and purpose being clarified and agreed in advance. If it was published every body involved would sign it or would be mentioned by name or collectively. If I had helped write any of it, I would sign it. Obviously, as in many situations certain children become more enthused about the finished product than others, but I'm always surprised at how keen children are to identify their own individual contributions.

> "It becomes a mixture of styles and voices."

I see this as very much linked to the above and I never find it a difficulty. Usually the reverse is true; the piece will take on a 'voice' as it gets going which children will respond to and develop. One of the wonderful things I find about shared writing is that the finished piece always seems to be better than anything that any individual in the class/group could have done on their own.

> "Some children don't join in so I feel it is a waste of their time."

I believe that first of all you have got to work at this. Shared writing has got to become a familair activity that children feel safe with and this obviously involves you creating the right kind of supportive atmosphere where chuildren feel their contributions, however small, are valued. You will be surprised how after a while children gain confidence from gentle encouragement, combined with the boost of seeing their idea incorporated into the writing. Some children may just prefer to listen but that doesn't mean that they are not taking in what's going on, quite the opposite. Many children benefit greatly from watching and listening. After all, while attending teachers' in-service courses not all teachers feel inclined to contribute to brainstorming sessions using a flip chart, but this doesn't mean that they're not reflecting on the contributions of the others who do!

Another important issue to remember is that shared writing is not an 'exclusive' form. Try combining it. Share-write a beginning for children to finish individually. Or, for example, take a story a child has written, where they are not happy with their ending, and share-write an ending together.

> "Children don't listen; they get bored."

If children switch off it may be time to stop and do something else and come back to it for a short session later. Don't be frightened to abandon a session altogether if it is not working. Keep things very tight and structured if children are new to shared writing. Have clear goals and purposes that children can appreciate (e.g. writing and designing a publicity poster for the school bookshop).

It's an idea to vary your shared writing sessions and liven things up with the odd "How do you spell that word?" or "Can you think of another word which ends in 'able'?" for example. Encourage children to think of synonms e.g. "I can think of another word that means the same thing beginning with d". Pitch the questions you ask at different levels – some children enjoy being picked on to answer questions, it helps keep others interested!

In my experience if groups are too small it's hard for shared writing to feel lively and inspirational. I would recommend a minimum of 8 children and would personally prefer a whole class any day!

> "I don't like selecting and rejecting childrens' individual contributions."

The reality is that you have to but it's also something that the children will be doing themselves during the shared writing. If necessary take several alternative suggestions from different children and get the group to decide on the one they think is best. Top juniors are very discerning!

Some children need to be more selective with their own contributions and not necessarily 'brainstorm' or shout out the first thing that comes into their heads. For those children I always feel that shared writing can be very helpful. Of course it's important to create an atmosphere where children will not worry if their ideas are rejected. Children need to be encouraged to shape their thoughts before sharing them, without being overly worried about getting it perfect – it's a difficult balance!

Using Shared Writing as a Technique for Helping Children with Poetry Writing

I am frequently amazed and humbled by the capacity of many young children to write beautiful poetry, so much so that I often wonder what happens to make most children stop writing poetry later in life. On the other hand I am always concious of those children who, like me as a child, find it enormously difficult. It was partly my lack of confidence in how best to help children to write better poetry that prompted me to experiment with shared writing as a technique.

To encourage children to write poetry, it is essential that they are given many opportunities to read and listen to poetry themselves. Even so, for many, it is still a daunting and inaccessible world. Explaining the process to children (e.g. using the best words in the best order) is equally as daunting for teachers!

I have found that writing a communal poem as a shared writing activity can be an excellent way of modelling poetry writing for a group of children. Initially this can involve fair amounts of teacher input, and help if necessary, in order that children grasp ideas which will help their own development as poetry writers.

● Don't be over reluctant to make your own contributions to a piece of shared writing. You can be one of the joint authors! In fact it is not always possible to be purely the scribe and make no contributions without the session becoming disappointing or unfocussed. The skill is in making timely interventions that spark off further ideas. You could try getting a competent speller to share being the scribe with you and then you can sit back and join in with the children. Giving yourselves a defined task, which you make clear to everyone at the start, can also be useful. You may want to model a particular style or form of poetry or you may want to look closely at a particular poem, re-writing it or adapting its form to a different topic.

● Of course, it's not just shared poetry writing that gives rise to genuine opportunities to discuss the suitability of a word or phrase. Yet I always feel that considering alternatives, and playing around with selecting particular words, is most clearly illustrated and encouraged with shared poetry writing. I always feel that a teacher modelling the processes that all writers go through in a shared writing situation is a very effective use of teacher time.

● An important part of poetry writing is reworking and editing, but for many children this is a difficult and seemingly unnecessary thing to do. Some children can produce a perfect piece first time around, while others need extensive help with the editing or with mistakes. With shared writing, editing can be a small or major part of the process. The routine surface editing that you do immediately you have finished writing alone, you tend to do as you go along with shared writing. Any obvious mistakes you make as you scribe are always spotted immediately! At the end when you read through there is the opportunity to discuss punctuation, paragraphs and other surface features, such as the obvious repetition of a word that sounds clumsy. However, it is for the "revising and rewriting" sort of editing that shared writing can be such a powerful tool. Remember you don't always need to make major changes, the initial and simplest thoughts are often the best. Or, as can often happen with poetry, you may have been reshaping and rewriting pretty much as you go along.

I wouldn't want to recommend the Donald Graves approach with shared writing, certainly the thought of multiple drafts of a piece of shared writing are enough to put any child or teacher off! Reworking a piece of writing is not a process that comes easily to children or one they always see as necessary and I've always found it frustratingly

difficult to deal with when 'conferencing' a piece of writing with a child individually. Apart from asking the child sensitive questions which may prompt them into suggesting changes themselves, I feel it is rather an imposition and even demoralising for a child to be obliged to go and rewrite a text. But I do believe that anything which can encourage children to look critically at a piece of composition and see the possibilities and benefits of rewriting is extremely useful. Shared writing is such a thing. With a large group of children there will be considerable selecting and rejecting of words and phrases and that can become part of the fun.

Then of course comes the final proof-reading and deciding how the poem is going to be published. Perhaps it will be read in assembly, be part of a class anthology to be published as a small illustrated book, put on the computer, or made into a wall display by child or teacher.

Shared Poetry Writing – some suggestions for getting started

Sometimes *taking a well known poem* and rewriting it, perhaps for a different audience or in a different style, can be a very worth while shared writing activity. There is nothing wrong with taking a well known poem and trying to encourage children to write a poem copying the same style or format. Kenneth Koch's book *Rose, How Did you get that Red*, is a wonderful example of using this kind of starting point.

Re-writing an extended narrative poem can be a wonderful collaborative exercise. Agree beforehand on the purpose of the task (e.g. to shorten and simplify the original, make it more suitable for a contempory audience, re-write in a different perhaps more direct style, get rid of the rhyme but retain the richness of language, change the ending etc.). I have used Alfred Noyes *The Highwayman* on many occasions with different

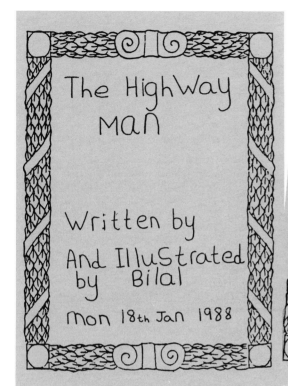

The Highway Man

Written by And Illustrated by Bilal

Mon 18th Jan 1988

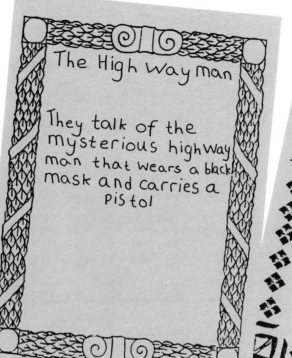

The Highway man

They talk of the mysterious highway man that wears a black mask and carries a pistol

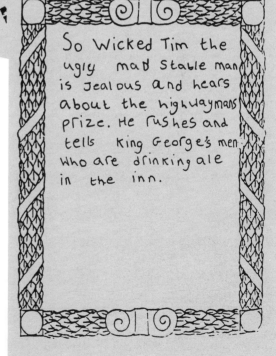

He comes and knocks at the old inn door and there stands the landlords black-eyed daughter with long, wavy hair. He had come to give his word that he would get his prize before the rising of the sun and would share the prize with the black-eyed daughter.

So Wicked Tim the ugly mad stable man is jealous and hears about the highwaymans prize. He rushes and tells King George's men who are drinking ale in the inn.

groups of children and never get tired of it. Although the language is not easy the story is so powerful that even young juniors are gripped. I have used it with groups of bilingual children inexperienced in English too and found that my expectations were not high enough; they showed greater feel for language and richness of style than I had anticipated.

On one occasion, working with 3rd year juniors, we read the poem several times then broke the narrative into distinct episodes. We wrote the first two together and then worked in pairs or threes on an episode each. I then pieced it all together and gave everybody a copy of the 'un-revised' piece and we worked on it together making final corrections, changes, looking at overall style and making sure it was all coherent and also looked closely at layout and punctuation. Finally children wrote the final two 'episodes' individually and made their own book of the whole poem with illustrations; the copying out was used for handwriting practise.

Another long narrative poem that I have used is *The Lady of Shalott* by Tennyson, using the version illustrated by Charles Keeping. It is a more difficult poem but I have used it with third years. We aimed to produce something more accessible and modern. We started off by breaking the story into manageable episodes to remind ourselves not just of the plot but also of the necessary scene setting etc. There was some disagreement, but it was decided not to use rhyme because it would be too difficult and restrictive. We also decided to use a long stanza for each 'episode' which the children called parts (the original is divided into four parts.) A concession to those who wanted a rhyme was to end each part with either "Camelot" or "Shalott", rather like the original. I remember that this poem needed very little editing at the end because all the selecting and rejecting and arguing was done as we went along.

Prose poetry form can free children from the convention of sentence construction, and of course rhyme, and therefore the child's authentic 'voice' is more likely to come through. Children can play

around with words and express themselves more freely. However much you read this kind of poetry to your class it will always be a very hard and often paralysing task for some children to write their own. As a way in, shared writing can be used to give children confidence and ideas before trying their own. However to help certain children you may still initially need to use a very real structure or even a model in your shared writing.

An *Acrostic poem*, where the first letters of each line make up a word, provides a distinct limit in terms of quantity and will break down the initial fear of the blank page. A five line *cinquain* is another possible form.

The very simple but regular form of the 17 syllable Japanese Haiku with three lines of five, seven, and five syllables respectively provides a manageable and enjoyable model for children to try. Another idea is to take an *unusual structure*, such as the poetry of William Carlos Williams, and get children to have a go themselves. In all of these cases you could have a go at shared writing initially before children write individually, hopefully with more confidence and more ideas.

Finally, if you haven't had a go at shared writing before I recommend you keep sessions short, simple and very structured to start with. Aim to turn the shared writing into a book or display it as soon as possible so the children are made very aware of its importance. "Poems on the tube" provide a good model for this. And of course, to develop children's poetry-writing you need to read them lots of poetry! This isn't difficult, poems are elastic. They can be squeezed into an odd five minute slot in the day or expand to fill a whole reading session.

Helen Kerslake
William Tyndale Primary School

Big Books
Norris Bentham

Don Holdaway's Foundations of Literacy makes it clear that the enlarged texts used in the New Zealand classrooms he describes were all teacher made. At one point, he writes that "publishers would soon meet this need if a general demand were voiced, but in the interim teachers have to back their convictions with ingenuity and hard labour.' A demand must have been voiced speedily, before the book was published in fact, for we find a note to Chapter 4 referring to Ashton Scholastic's Read-it-Again series which comprised large books, small versions and teachers' notes providing 'simple guidance for shared book experience teaching.' The notes were written by Libby Handy and Holdaway himself.

Scholastic in the U.K. brought these to British teachers soon after. They are long out of print, and while Scholastic have produced others since none of the titles are available at present.

Other publishers followed however, although considerably later, and many reading schemes now come with some of their books for beginning readers in large format. Arnold-Wheaton's Story Chest (now published by Nelson) was one of the first, with the Read Together Books set enlarged – Mrs. Wishy Washy being a notable success.

Of course, there is nothing about a poor text which is improved by making it larger and one can only hope that children will not have to suffer the limp text, the vacuous story or the constantly-repeated-one-word-text, just because the book is big.

Traditional stories, which incorporate many of the elements mentioned in the above article: rhyme, a cumulative text and meaningful repetition, are often the most successful and the following list gives some titles which teachers have found useful. Careful selection is necessary in view of the cost, which can go up to £20. Luckily, there is one initiative to which a wholehearted welcome can be given. Oliver & Boyd have published enlarged versions – in a more manageable size than most others – of some tried and tested titles, including the wonderful Ahlberg's Each Peach Pear Plum and Tony Ross's Oscar Got the Blame. Such an obvious thing to do, yet it took so long for anyone to think of it.

Norris Bentham
CLPE

Big Books List

The price and ISBN is for a single copy of the large book. A pack of large books, small versions and sometimes teachers notes is often available. Telephone numbers of publishers is given for obtaining full details, catalogues, etc.

Oliver & Boyd (0279 26721)

Storytime Giants

Janet and Allen Ahlberg
Each Peach Pear Plum   0 05 004406 0 £7.50

Ronda and David Armitage
The Lighthouse Keeper's Lunch   0 05 004387 0 £7.50
The Bossing of Josie   0 05 004388 9 £7.50

Mary Dickenson and Charlotte Firmin
Alex's Bed   0 05 004389 7 £7.50

Mary Dickenson and Joanna Stubbs
Jilly Takes Over   0 05 004510 5 £7.50

Susanna Gretz and Alison Sage
Teddybears Take the Train   0 05 004390 0 £7.50

Ruth Brown
The Big Sneeze   0 05 004391 9 £7.50

Phillipe Dupasquier
Daddy Dear   0 05 004392 7 £6.95

Mairi Hedderwick
Katie Morag and the Two Grandmothers
0 05 0044079 9 £7.50

Shirley Hughes
Lucy and Tom's Christmas   0 05 004509 1 £7.50

David McKee
Two Monsters   0 05 004546 6 £7.50

Tony Ross
Oscar Got the Blame   0 05 004405 2 £6.95

36

Rhymes to Remember

A collection of traditional rhymes

Mary Glasgow Publications (0926 640606)

Rhymes to Remember   1 85234 0770
A collection of traditional rhymes

The Great Invention   1 85234 0835
Rhyming text featuring a girl using assorted
material and tools to make a boat.
The Strange Loud Noise   1 85234 0835

A boy will not listen to an old lady trying to tell him
what the 'strange loud noise' is. The story is
cumulative as each possible source of the noise is
discounted and added to a list.

Ten Little Boats   1 85234 079 7
A rhyme based on the pattern of *'Ten Green Bottles'*
£7.95 each

Heinemann Educational (0933 58521)

Sunshine Books – *All-Together Books*
Margaret Mahy has written four delightful 'My
Wonderful Aunt' stories about a remarkable lady
who is

　　'too wild and free to reside in a house
　　So she lived in a hole
　　Like a rabbbit or a mouse'

The text rhymes throughout

Story One   0 435 00246 5
Story Two   0 435 00247 3
Story Three   0 435 00248 1
Story Four   0 435 00249 X

Further titles in the series are

'Wizard and the Rainbow'   0 435 00251 1
'A Wizard Came to Visit'   0 435 00250 3

£7.95 each

Hodder & Stoughton (0732 450111)

Hattie and the Fox by Mem Fox illustrated Patricia Mullins
0 340 48519 1 £9.95

Hattie the hen sees a fox's nose as it emerges from the bushes, then two ears then two eyes ————. At each stage other farmyard animals make the same uninterested comments, so there is plenty of meaningful repetition. Finally the fox emerges, the animals panic – only the cow moos loudly and frightens away the fox.

Hot Hippo by Mivenye Hadithi illustrated Adrienne Kennaway
0 340 48624 4 £9.95

Great story set in Africa explaining why the hippo opens his mouth so wide. Beautiful illustrations, more complex language.

Nelson (0932 246133)

Story Chest Books (formerly published by Arnold Wheaton)

1. Big Book versions of the Read Together books £9.95 each

2. Maths Rhyme Books – seven titles published so far £10.50 each

Each book contains several rhymes, represents excellent value for money and provides starting points for maths work.

Time for a Rhyme   0 1700 6161 2 £18.95
Time for a Number Rhyme   0 1700 6296 1 £20.95

Collections of nursery and other traditional rhymes.
Small versions of both these books are also available.

Schofield & Sims (0484 607080)

I Like This Book   0 7217 0516 2 £39.50

38

Tadpoles Books (01 741 8011)

Giant Books
A series of traditional Tales e.g.

The Three Billy Goats Gruff   0 7312 0033 0 £14.95
The Gingerbread Man   0 454 014 813 £14.95
and
Caterpillar Diary   0 454 01472 4
Tadpole Diary   0 454 04161 9 £14.95 each

Both these diaries feature beautiful close-up photographs. The text describes the development of tadpole and caterpillar stage by stage.

Stanley Thornes and Hulton (0242 228888)

When Goldilocks Went to the House of the Bears
illustrated Jenny Rendall   0 85950 787 4
A large version of the well-known song.

Interruptions Bronwen Scarffe and Diane Snowball   0 85950 788 2
Rhymes based on neighbours' names – a good model for children making their own version.

When the King Rides By Margaret Mahy
illustrated Bettina Ogden
0 85950 809 9
A cumulative rhyme about the fuss made when a king rides by.

The Old Man's Mitten Yevonne Pollock
0 85950 808 0
A traditional tale about a collection of animals who one by one make their home in an old man's mitten – until they hear the old man's dog bark. Plenty of repetition.   £10.00 each

Display

Although it is perfectively possible to adapt old easels, clothes 'horses' etc. for displaying big books, there are available special display stands from the following suppliers:

Tadpole Books   01 743 8011 about £28.00
Top Stone   05827 64510 about £20.00
E.J. Arnold   0532 772112 about £34.00
Philip & Tacy   0264 332171 A table stand £7.60

Norris Bentham
Gillian Lathey

Contributors

Rehana Alam is now Induction Coordinator for the London Borough of Tower Hamlets. She was previously a member of the ILEA Unified Language Service.

Norris Bentham is the librarian at CLPE. She edits the Reviews section of *Language Matters* and has contributed to several CLPE publications.

Helen Kerslake is deputy head teacher of William Tyndale Primary School, London Borough of Islington. Previously she was a primary teacher and an advisory teacher with ILEA. She has contributed to *Language Matters*.

Gillian Lathey is a senior lecturer at Roehampton Institute of Higher Education. She has worked as an infant teacher and an advisory teacher for Language in the National Curriculum in ILEA and in the London Borough of Islington. She is a member of the NATE 0-11 committee.

Liz Laycock is a senior lecturer and the Language Teaching Studies Area Coordinator at Roehampton Institute of Higher Education. She worked as a primary teacher and an advisory teacher in ILEA and has frequently contributed to *Language Matters*.

Audrey Ringrose is an infant teacher at Annandale Primary School, London Borough of Greenwich. She has contributed to *Language Matters*.

Sue Pidgeon lectures in primary education at Goldsmiths College, University of London. She has been a primary teacher with ILEA and a reading advisory teacher with CLPE. She has contributed to *Language Matters* and to other CLPE publications, including *Read, Read, Read*.

Penny Tuxford and Anne Washtell taught together in the infant department of Wix Primary School, London Borough of Wandsworth, for eight years. Both have contributed to *Language Matters*, and have given courses on early writing at CLPE. Penny Tuxford has been a visiting lecturer at Roehampton Institute of Education; Anne Washtell is a senior lecturer at R.I.H.E. and has published in the journal *Language Arts* (NCTE).